For Amelia and Garrett, with love—K. S. D.

For Dénes, Mosi, and Orsi—M. O.

BEACH LANE BOOKS

An imprint of Simon & Schuster Children's Publishing Division
1230 Avenue of the Americas, New York, New York 10020
Text copyright © 2020 by Katy S. Duffield
Illustrations copyright © 2020 by Mike Orodán
All rights reserved, including the right of reproduction in whole or in part in any form.
BEACH LANE BOOKS is a trademark of Simon & Schuster, Inc.
For information about special discounts for bulk purchases, please contact Simon & Schuster Special Sales at 1-866-506-1949
or business@simonandschuster.com.
The Simon & Schuster Speakers Bureau can bring authors to your live event. For more information or to book an event,
contact the Simon & Schuster Speakers Bureau at 1-866-248-3049 or visit our website at www.simonspeakers.com.
Book design by Lauren Rille
The text for this book was set in Vicky.
The illustrations for this book were rendered by hand with graphite pencils and Adobe Photoshop.
Manufactured in China
0720 SCP
First Edition
10 9 8 7 6 5 4 3 2 1
Library of Congress Cataloging-in-Publication Data • Names: Duffield, Katy, author. | Orodan, Mike, illustrator. • Title: Crossings / Katy S.
Duffield ; illustrated by Mike Orodan. • Description: First edition. | New York : Beach Lane Books, an imprint of Simon & Schuster Children's
Publishing Division, 2020. | Audience: Ages 3–8. | Audience: Grades 2–3. | Summary: "A nonfiction exploration of animal crossings built
by animal lovers around the world to help animals cross over, under, around, and through human construction"—Provided by publisher.
• Identifiers: LCCN 2019053820 (print) | ISBN 9781534465794 (hardcover) | ISBN 9781534465800 (eBook) • Subjects: LCSH: Wildlife
crossings—Juvenile literature. | Wildlife conservation—Juvenile literature. | Conservation projects (Natural resources)—Juvenile literature.
| Animals—Effect of roads on—Juvenile literature. • Classification: LCC SK356.W54 D84 2020 (print) | DDC 333.95/4—dc23 • LC record
available at https://lccn.loc.gov/2019053820

Written by
Katy S. Duffield

Illustrated by
Mike Orodán

CROSSINGS

EXTRAORDINARY STRUCTURES FOR EXTRAORDINARY ANIMALS

Beach Lane Books
New York   London   Toronto   Sydney   New Delhi

Over, under, across, through. Around the world, construction crews build overpasses, underpasses, bridges, and tunnels— ways for people to get from one place to another.

But what about the animals that live in these places?

What happens when construction spreads
over, under, across, and through their habitats?

Around the world, in search of solutions,
animal lovers come together.

Over.

Under.

Across.

Through.

Opening their minds
and their hearts, they work
to find ideas, answers.

Construction crews work again.
But *these* structures aren't for
traveling people.

They're for traveling animals.

A bull elk picks his way through evergreens OVER a noisy Canadian highway.

The Trans-Canada Highway is home to more than forty wildlife overpasses and underpasses. And the crossings don't just benefit elk. Bears, wolves, cougars, bighorn sheep, and other animals use the crossings too.

A mama elephant thunders UNDER
a crowded Kenyan road.

For many years, two groups of elephants—
one from Mount Kenya's highlands and another
from the plains and forests below—have been
separated by a major highway. But with the
addition of an elephant underpass, the two
groups can now reconnect and share habitats.

Squirrel gliders skitter ACROSS woven rope bridges stretched high above an Australian freeway.

Hume Highway, used by about ten thousand vehicles per day, was an extremely hazardous route for squirrel gliders. But now, thanks to the addition of rope bridges above the busy road, squirrel gliders can cross safely to breed and to find food.

Blue penguins hustle home
to their chicks THROUGH
a tiny tunnel beneath the
New Zealand pavement.

The blue penguins of Oamaru travel to the sea for food, but nest on the land. At sunset, the birds were forced to cross a busy road to get back to the chicks in their nests—until a lighted underpass was built to assist them. And once they discovered the safe crossing, the little birds made it their daily route.

Red crabs scuttle up, up, and OVER an Australian bridge that leads to the Indian Ocean.

Every year, sometime between October and January, millions of red crabs leave the forests of Christmas Island and head for the Indian Ocean, where female crabs will lay their eggs. Specially built crab bridges help keep the brightly colored crustaceans out of harm's way on their journeys.

Florida panthers slip, slink
UNDER the roar of traffic above.

Over time, the Florida panthers' habitat has dwindled to almost nothing. Wildlife crossings help keep the animals away from the dangers of the roadways and open up broader areas for these endangered animals to grow and thrive.

Titi monkeys tightrope ACROSS blue rope bridges that keep them safe above a Costa Rican road.

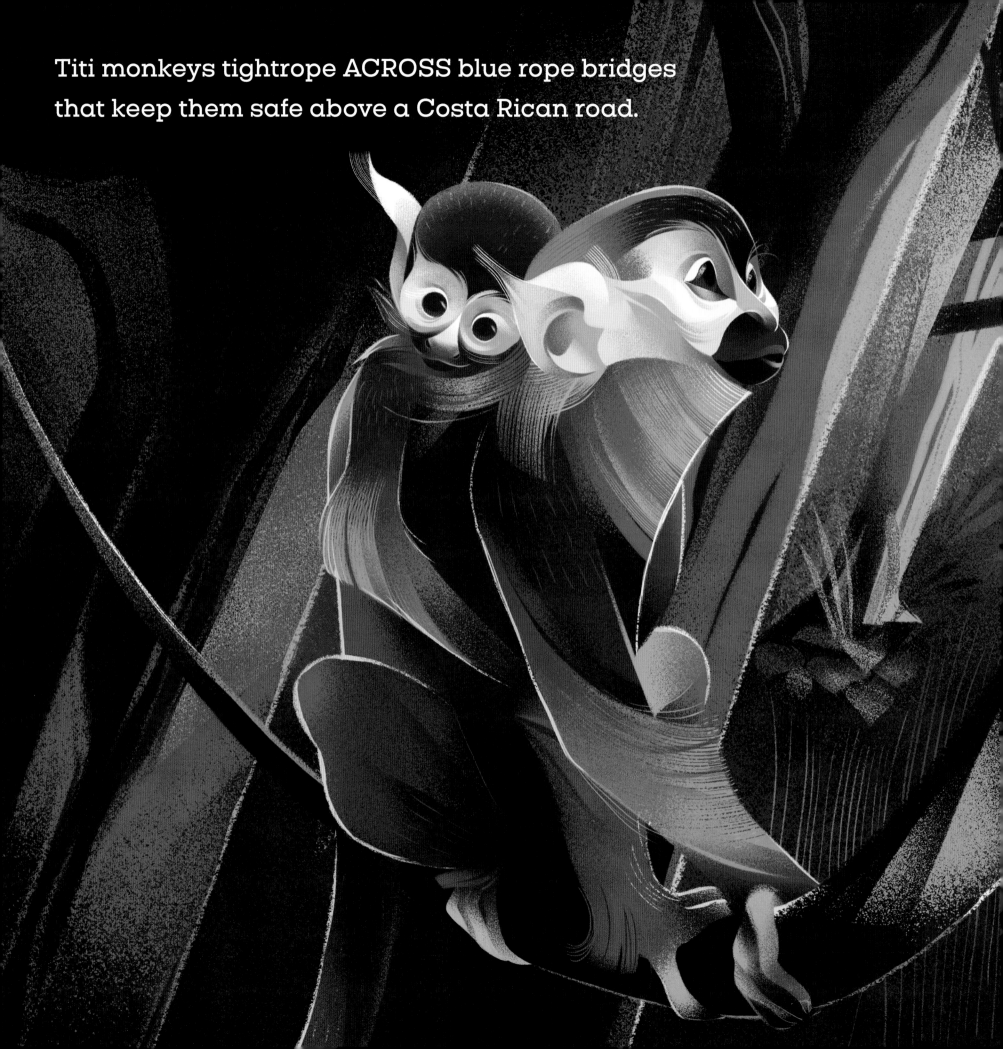

Costa Rica's smallest species of monkey, the titi, is endangered. A group of young people, Kids Saving the Rainforest, found a solution to help save them: thick blue ropes strung across roads enable the monkeys to move safely from one side to the other.

Spotted salamanders shimmy THROUGH peewee passageways beneath a Massachusetts street.

Each spring, as evening temperatures begin to rise, spotted salamanders in North Amherst head for the ponds where they will breed. Tiny crossings, aided by fencing to guide the little guys, were installed to help keep their travels safe.

Coyotes creep OVER the rush
of Arizona motorists below.

Coyotes and many other animals, including javelinas, bobcats, rabbits, quail, deer, foxes, roadrunners, and skunks, use the crossings in Arizona.

Black bear cubs follow Mama
UNDER a Montana highway.

Before wildlife crossings were built on Highway 93 in Montana, engineers teamed up with biologists to search for the perfect place to build the crossings. They used sand pits to record animal footprints and even counted poop piles to discover the animals' favorite crossing spots.

Pangolins teeter-totter toward their burrows
ACROSS a Singapore expressway.

When the Bukit Timah Expressway in Singapore was built, it cut a wide swath of rainforest in two. The busy six-lane roadway kept critically endangered Sunda pangolins from food, shelter, and mates. But today the hourglass-shaped wildlife bridge helps them safely find their way to the other side.

A koala saunters THROUGH a tunnel,
along a ledge, below an Australian road.

Koalas can swim, but prefer to keep their feet dry—
a problem for crossings in low areas that can be full
of water. To entice the furry marsupials to use the
underpasses, workers added ledges and logs that act
as bridges above the wet ground.

Over.

Under.

Across.

Through.

Around the world, these
unique structures protect animals—

living proof that opening
our minds, and our hearts,
can make all the difference.

Wildlife Crossings Around the World

Kenya: Elephants
The fifteen-foot-high tunnel that sits below Mount Kenya is believed to be the first elephant underpass built in Africa. To attract the elephants to the tunnel, workers lined the ground beneath it with hay and elephant dung. And their efforts paid off! Within a few weeks of its opening, a bull elephant named Tony made the first trek beneath the road.

Singapore: Sunda Pangolins
To help shy Sunda pangolins and other animals feel at home on the Bukit Timah Expressway crossing, 3,000 trees and shrubs were planted to entice the animals to make their way across the wildlife bridge.

Australia: Koalas
When searching for ways to keep koalas safe from traffic, experts believed that overpasses might not work. Koalas often don't feel secure in the open, so researchers created underpasses that worked perfectly for the temperament of the furry marsupials.

Christmas Island, Australia: Red Crabs
Adult crabs aren't the only ones using the crab bridge. When they are old enough, baby crabs leave the ocean waters and journey along the same route that their parents took. But instead of going toward the sea, the babies head inland where they hide, live, and grow until they are big enough to venture out.

Australia: Squirrel Gliders
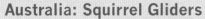
Over the years, land around northeast Victoria has steadily been cleared for farming. This clearing cost Australia's squirrel gliders much of their treetop habitat. The only big trees left, those containing special hollows where squirrel gliders like to nest, were located near roadsides and the busy Hume Highway, leading to increased danger for the animals. Now rope bridges help keep them safe.

New Zealand: Blue Penguins
Blue penguins, also known as little penguins or fairy penguins, are the world's smallest penguins. The tiny birds have been in decline, but officials are continually looking for new ways to build up their numbers, and the tunnel crossing in Oamaru has been one "waddle" in the right direction.

Trans-Canada Highway, Banff National Park: Elk

To help elk and other animals find their way across the highway, fencing is installed in some areas to guide the animals toward the wildlife crossings. Elk were the first large animals to use the Banff crossings. Some even made the trip across while the crossings were still under construction!

Montana, USA: Black Bears

A section of US Highway 93 in northwestern Montana is home to more than forty wildlife crossings—the majority of which are various types of underpasses. Black bears, grizzly bears, mountain lions, moose, elk, river otters, and other animals have been filmed or photographed using the underpasses.

Massachusetts, USA: Spotted Salamanders

The ten-inch-high, six-inch-wide crossings, built along Henry Street in North Amherst, have slotted tops to allow moisture into tunnels. Dampness is important for the spotted salamanders. It helps the estimated 100–200 amphibians that cross beneath the road each year to keep from drying out on their journeys.

Arizona, USA: Coyotes

Game cameras snap photos of animals as they cross the Arizona overpasses and underpasses, and some animals can be a little picky about what type of crossing they use. While coyotes don't seem to have a preference, javelinas and bobcats prefer using underpasses, while most deer prefer to take the "high road" of the overpasses.

Florida, USA: Florida Panthers

Housing and other types of development have forced Florida panthers into smaller and smaller areas of land. Since estimates show that the population of these big cats ranges roughly between 100 and 200 animals, underpasses can provide a safe way for the skittish animals to get from one area to another to reproduce and increase their numbers.

Costa Rica: Titi Monkeys

The numbers of Costa Rica's titi monkey, also known as the Central American squirrel monkey, had dropped to fewer than 4,000 animals. But thanks to more than 125 rope bridges, the monkeys' population has been increasing.

Selected bibliography and further reading:

Cullinane, Susannah. "NZ Builds Underpass for Little Penguins to Safely Cross Road." CNN.com. November 12, 2016. https://www.cnn.com/2016/11/12/asia/nz-penguin-underpass/index.html

Debczak, Michele. "7 Animal Crossings Around the World." Mental Floss. March 3, 2020. https://www.mentalfloss.com/article/618976/animal-crossings-around-the-world

Ries, Olivia. "Monkey Bridges for Everyone." National Geographic Education Blog. May 18, 2016. https://blog.education.nationalgeographic.org/2016/05/18/monkey-bridges-for-everyone/

Vartan, Starre. "How Wildlife Bridges over Highways Make Animals—and People—Safer." NationalGeographic.com. April 16, 2019. https://www.nationalgeographic.com/animals/2019/04/wildlife-overpasses-underpasses-make-animals-people-safer/

Parks Canada. "Wildlife Crossing Structures and Research Frequently Asked Questions." Banff National Park. Updated April 1, 2017. https://www.pc.gc.ca/en/pn-np/ab/banff/info/gestion-management/enviro/transport/tch-rtc/passages-crossings/faq

To view videos of animals using wildlife crossings, visit KatyDuffield.com.